Animals on Land

Animals Do What?

By Brenda McHale

Published in 2023 by Enslow Publishing, LLC
29 East 21st Street, New York, NY 10010

© 2022 Booklife Publishing
This edition is published by arrangement with
Booklife Publishing

Edited by:
Emilie Dufresne

Designed by:
Dan Scase

All rights reserved. No part of this book may be reproduced in any form without permission in writing from the publisher, except by a reviewer.

Manufactured in the United States of America

CPSIA compliance information: Batch #CSENS23. For further information contact Enslow Publishing LLC, New York, New York at 1-800-398-2504.

Please visit our website, www.enslowpublishing.com.
For a free color catalog of all our high-quality books, call toll free 1-800-398-2504 or fax 1-877-980-4454.

Find us on

Cataloging-in-Publication Data

Names: McHale, Brenda.
Title: Animals on land / Brenda McHale.
Description: New York : Enslow Publishing, 2023. | Series: Animals do what? | Includes glossary and index.
Identifiers: ISBN 9781978531383 (pbk.) | ISBN 9781978531406 (library bound) | ISBN 9781978531390 (6 pack) | ISBN 9781978531413 (ebook)
Subjects: LCSH: Animals--Juvenile literature.
Classification: LCC QL49.M343 2023 | DDC 590--dc23

PHOTO CREDITS

All images are courtesy of Shutterstock.com. With thanks to Getty Images, Thinkstock Photo and iStockphoto. Front page – Opayaza12. 4&5 – prapass, asawinimages, Dirk Ercken. 6&7 – Silvia Pascual, Rene Baars, Anton_Ivanov, BMJ. 8&9 – Valdis Skudre, Linda Marie Caldwell, BlueOrange Studio, Wim Hoek. 10&11 – apple2499, Eric Isselee, rickyd. 12&13 – John Carnemolla, BEJITA, khlungcenter. 14&15 – janusz.kol, Dirk Ercken, Tsekhmister, Smith. 16&17 – Vladimir Chernyanskiy, Inna Ska, nomad-photo.eu, DioGen. 18&19 – Agami Photo Agency, Vitalii Hulai, Sakdinon Kadchiangsaen. 20&21 – Dr Morley Read, LukaKikina. 22&23 – Villiers Steyn, fred goldstein, Ondrej Prosicky, Mandy Creighton, Viktor Loki, Dirk Daniel Mann.

CONTENTS

PAGE 4	What Lives on the Land?
PAGE 6	Penguin
PAGE 8	Giraffe
PAGE 10	Koala
PAGE 12	Termite
PAGE 14	Frog
PAGE 16	Hedgehog
PAGE 18	Dung Beetle
PAGE 20	Stick Insect
PAGE 22	Bonus Beasts
PAGE 24	Glossary and Index

Words that look like <u>this</u> can be found in the glossary on page 24.

WHAT LIVES ON THE LAND?

There are lots of crazy creatures that live on land. Here are some of the types of animals that you can find there...

Insects such as millipedes

Mammals such as zebras

Amphibians such as tree frogs

TREE FROG

Type: Amphibian
Found: South and Central America
Diet: Flies, ants, and other invertebrates

On each page you will see a fact file like this. It will give you cool facts about the animal, such as what type of animal it is, its diet, and where it lives.

PENGUIN

Emperor penguins can stay underwater for 20 minutes. They slow their heartbeat so that they use up less <u>energy</u>.

PENGUIN
Type: <u>Bird</u>
Found: <u>Below the equator</u>
Diet: Fish and other sea creatures

Penguins live both on the land and in the water.

Large amounts of penguin poop can be seen from space. Scientists use this information to find out where penguins are on land.

Penguins that live on the ice in Antarctica have to huddle together during winter. Huddling in a big group keeps each penguin warm.

Penguins sneeze and shake their heads to get rid of any salt that they swallow while swimming in seawater.

GIRAFFE

A giraffe's long neck only has seven bones, the same as ours! Their bones are a lot bigger than ours.

GIRAFFE

Type: Mammal
Found: African savanna
Diet: Leaves and twigs

They spread their legs wide to bend down to drink. Luckily, they only drink every few days!

Giraffes can be up to 20 feet (6 m) tall. That is taller than a double-decker bus!

Every giraffe's markings are different, like our fingerprints.

They sometimes chew on the bones of dead animals, even though they don't eat the meat.

KOALA

Koalas are <u>marsupials</u>.

KOALA

Type: Mammal
Found: Australia
Diet: Eucalyptus leaves

Koalas mostly eat the leaves of eucalyptus trees and almost nothing else.

They hardly ever drink. They get most of the water they need from the eucalyptus leaves they eat.

Koala fingerprints are very similar to human fingerprints.

Koalas sleep for 20 hours a day. They eat for up to four hours a day. That means they can spend the whole day just eating and sleeping.

Koalas have tiny brains for their size compared to other marsupials.

TERMITE

TERMITE

Type: Insect
Found: Everywhere but Antarctica
Diet: Plants

Some termites build huge mounds above their underground nests. The mound helps keep the air in the nest cool and fresh.

Termites fart a lot! Tiny living things in their mounds help to break down their farts.

FROG

A group of frogs is called an army.

A frog usually <u>sheds</u> its skin about once a week. Most times it will eat the old one. Ew!

FROG

Type: Amphibian
Found: Worldwide
Diet: Insects

The biggest frog in the world is the goliath frog. It can be the size of a human baby!

The glass frog has see-through skin. You can see its insides!

Male Darwin's frogs swallow their young and keep them in their mouth while they grow. They then burp out fully grown frogs!

HEDGEHOG

HEDGEHOG

Type: Mammal
Found: Forests, deserts, and gardens in Europe, Asia, Africa, and New Zealand
Diet: Small animals and plants

Hedgehogs grunt like pigs. Hog is another name for pig.

Hedgehogs can swim and even climb!

A hedgehog can walk around 2 miles (3.2 km) a night when looking for food. That's a long way for little legs!

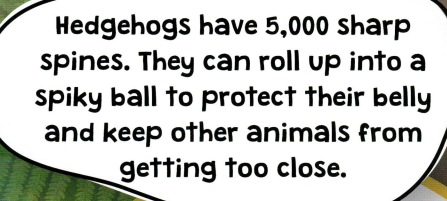

Hedgehogs have 5,000 sharp spines. They can roll up into a spiky ball to protect their belly and keep other animals from getting too close.

Hedgehogs can make themselves <u>poisonous</u>! They can eat plants that are poisonous to other animals. They chew them up, then rub their spit all over their spines!

DUNG BEETLE

DUNG BEETLE

Type: Insect
Found: Worldwide except Antarctica
Diet: Other animals' poop

Dung is another word for poop. Dung beetles love to eat poop!

Dung beetles find their way by using the stars as a map.

A dung beetle has been seen moving a ball of poop 1,000 times its body weight. That is like a person moving six full buses!

Some female dung beetles lay each egg in a nest inside a little ball of poop. When the egg hatches, the baby beetle eats the poop!

These beetles are hatching from their dung balls.

Balls of dung from beetles have been found as <u>fossils</u>. They were 30 million years old!

STICK INSECT

The Australian walking stick smells like peanut butter when it feels threatened.

Stick insects can <u>camouflage</u> themselves. These ones look like leaves.

They can break off a leg to escape an attacker. The next time they shed their skin, they grow another leg on the new skin.

STICK INSECT

Type: Insect
Found: Worldwide except Antarctica
Diet: Leaves

Stick insects can play dead. They fall off a tree and stay very still to confuse attackers.

There are two stick insects in this picture. Can you find them?

Some stick insects are tiny, but some are nearly as long as a child's arm.

BONUS BEASTS

Baby elephants suck their trunks just like human children suck their thumbs.

Sea otters hold hands while they sleep to keep them from floating away.

Flamingo feathers are turned pink by the shrimp they eat.

Wombat poop is cube shaped.

Wood frogs can freeze in the winter and their heart can stop beating, but they will still survive as the weather gets warmer.

Male ring-tailed lemurs fight by making a nasty smell. They wave their tails to waft it to the lemur they are fighting with!

GLOSSARY

amphibians	animals that can live both on land and in water
bird	an animal with feathers, two wings, and two feet
camouflage	to hide by blending in with surroundings
diet	the kinds of foods that a person or animal usually eats
energy	the power to make something work or do something
equator	the imaginary line around Earth that is an equal distance from the North and South Poles
fossils	parts of plants and animals from a long time ago that have been kept in good condition inside rocks
insects	animals with one or two pairs of wings, six legs, and no backbone
invertebrates	animals that do not have a backbone
mammals	animals that are warm-blooded, have a backbone, and produce milk to feed their young
marsupials	animals that are part of a group in which the females have a pouch outside their body to carry their young
poisonous	dangerous or deadly when eaten
sheds	removes and replaces the skin or shell with another one that has grown underneath

INDEX

amphibians 4–5, 14
babies 14–15, 19, 22
birds 6
brains 11

insects 4, 12, 14, 18, 20–21
mammals 4, 8, 10, 16
marsupials 10–11
nests 12–13, 19

poop 6, 18–19, 23
smells 20, 23
water 6–7, 10